Poems to Share with Someone You Know

Poems and drawings by Chester Black

Coldworthy
Writers Guild LLC

Copyright (May 21,2025) By Chester Black

All rights reserved. No part of this book may be reproduced, transmitted, or stored in an information retrieval system in any form or by any means, graphic, electronic, including photocopying, taping, and recording, without the prior written permission from the publisher, except where permitted by law.

ISBN: 979-8-9994902-1-6

The author has written many poems, on a variety of subjects. This is the authors second book of poems and illustrations. It was inspired by people he knows.

While reciting these poems the children in the audience told the author that the poem "Mother's Rules" was about their friend, or more often their brother.

The adults in the audience said they worked with the person who would, or should recite "(You Know Who's) Prayer",

This is a collection for the family, because everyone, young or old, will recognize a poem they will want to share with family or friend.

Thus, it's title "Poems to Share with Someone You Know"

Contents Page #

1 Mother's Rules

2 I Know It All

3 A Wet Kid

4 I Had a Wish

5 Autobiography

7 Baby Brother

9 Blocks

11 Chins

12 Dreams Can Come True

13 Crystal Ball

15 Cold's Name

16 Doodles

17 Eating Healthy

18 Empty Boxes

19 The Donkey & the Elephant

21 Firetruck

22 Old Friends

23 Grandpa's Stories

24 Is it Fair?

25 I Look at the Stars

26 Sleeping Cat

27 I Want to Fly

29 Lane in the Rain

30 Muddy Shoes

31 Sharing

33 May's Queen

35 My Hat

36 My Love Smiles

37 My Belt

39 Lady Chesterfield

41 My First Fair

43 Too Much Sun

44 Peanut Butter

45 Who Taught Him That

47 Neighborhood

48 Penguins

49 No Longer Lonely

50. (You Know Who's) Prayer

51 Rude Awakening

52 Shoes

53 Scary Eyes

54 My Shadow

55 My Kitten

56 Sharing

57 Getting Older

58 Socks

59 Be an Example

60 Sunrise

61 A Belt

63 Another Plea

65 Eulogy?

Mother's Rules

Your fingers are your most useful tools
But you must remember mother's rules
For your friends they must never close
And they must never ever go in your nose

I Know It All

I've been told it's a very sad day
When you don't learn something new
So, I've worked really hard to make sure
Those kinds of days were but few

Some days I've learned something big
Some days I've learned something small
But I've always tried to learn something
So, I can stop now, for I know it all

A Wet Kid

My puppy and I went for a walk
He's young so it's part of his training
We had only gotten about a block
When it suddenly started raining

"Let's get under cover" I started yelling
So, we quickly hid under a tree
I said "Like a wet dog you are now smelling"
He wrinkled his nose and sniffed at me

I Had a Wish

I had a wish

I wished to share

But just with who

Would I dare

Some might joke

Some might giggle

Fingers of old folk

Might just wiggle

I had a wish

It faded away

Maybe I'll have another

Some distant day

Autobiography

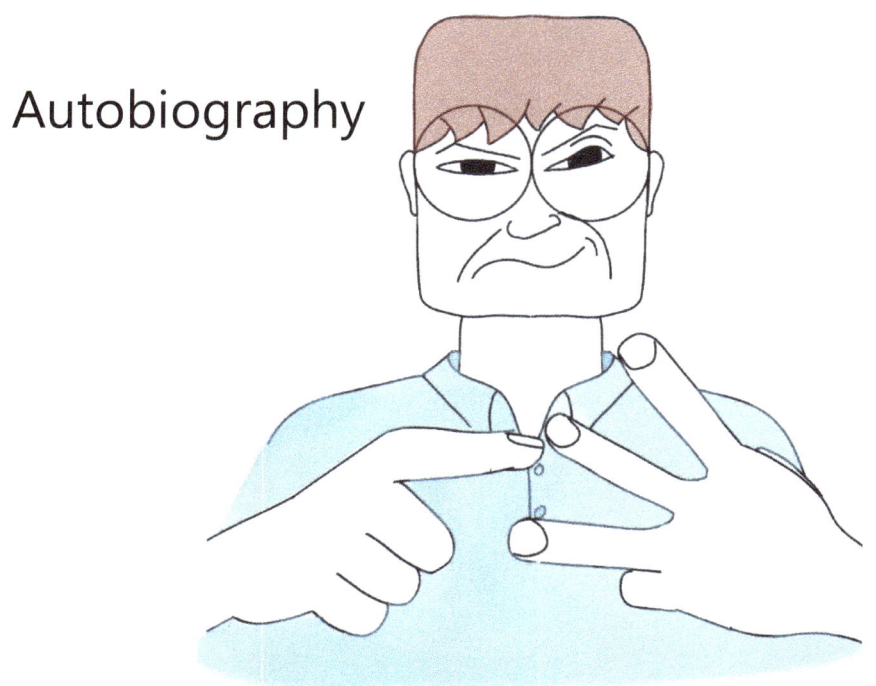

After he told his tale
I asked if it was a lie
He swore truth of every detail
Oh, really! was my reply

You said you walked at two
And started school at three
Then built your own house
At five up in a tree

You said ten years you spent
In the jungles of the tropics
And then ten years you went
To France to work on robotics

You also said you studied
For ten years in Tibet
And spent ten years muddied
in Vermont you'd like to forget

But the part of your story
That I questioned the most
Were the ten years you spent
In bed totally comatose

It is then I started to wonder
About the story you told
For that story covers fifty years
While you're only twenty years old

Baby Brother

Mother asked if a pony
Was my birthday wish she heard
She asked softly if I'd agree
A little brother might be preferred

I said "My friends' little brothers
Are always getting in the way
So, if I had my druthers
A pony my wish would stay"

Mother said "He'd be a baby
And would be oh so adorable
If I helped care for him, maybe
He would not be so horrible"

When Mother brought him home
He was the cutest, however
It was when he first smiled at me
I knew he was the best wish ever

Blocks

The toddler likes colored blocks
    and building towers sky high
He only smiles when he finally knocks
    all the steeples awry

He's building towers once again
    this time making them higher
He builds until no blocks remain
    then grins at the spire

All the blocks come cascading down
    with thuds and bangs galore
Laughter is replaced by a determined frown
    as he starts to build once more

Chins

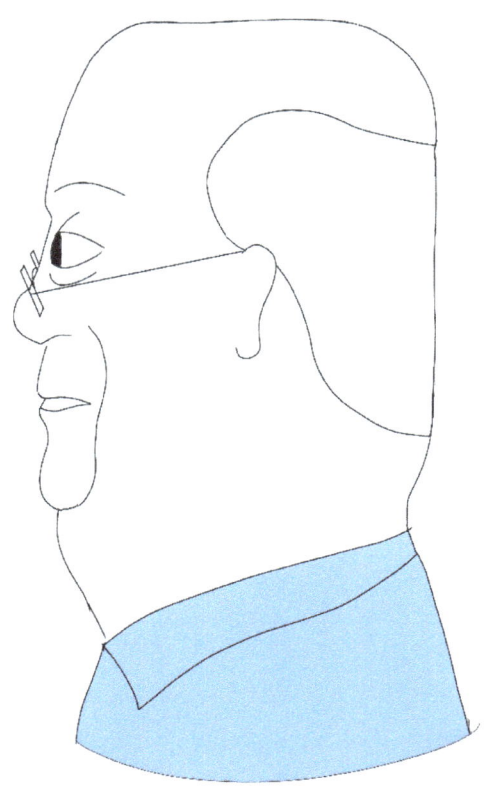

Chins can be pointy
Chins can be cleft
Chins can be hairy
Chins can have heft

I always liked mine
I've kept it up when troubled
I think it looks just fine
But I don't know when it doubled

Dreams Can Come True

Dream of leaders honest and true
Leaders that respect me and you

Dream of a community shiny and clean
With community gardens lush and green

Dream of the children attentive in class
It can all only come true if you get off your...

Crystal Ball

So many decisions to make
At night they keep me awake

If only there were just a few
And all of the answers I knew

My life would be calmer then
And I might sleep once again

But the longer I fret it seems
More worries haunt my dreams

What a blissful life it would be
If into the future I could see

Each right choice I foresaw
At worries I could guffaw

Oh, what price wouldn't I pay
To be able to sleep all night today

Cold's Name

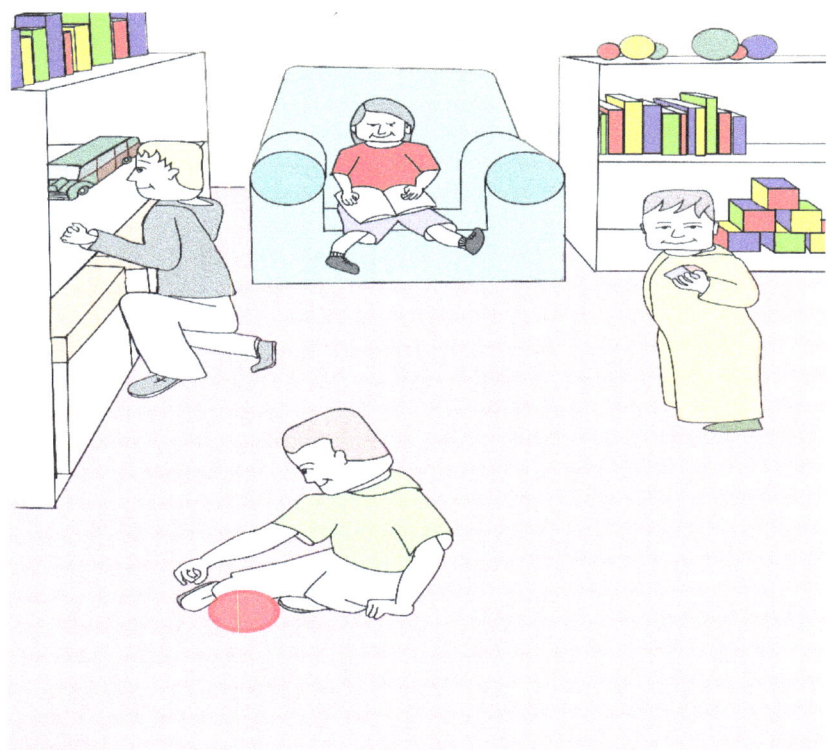

Just as the weathermen find it opportune
To name every hurricane and typhoon
I have decided that what I must do
Is name every cold, influenza, and flu
I think it's best if I give them the name
Of the last grandchild that to my house came
For although I want them to visit and set no terms
It's been my experience they always leave germs

Doodles

Doodles are scribbled
By fools like me
But only an artist
Can draw a tree

Eating Healthy

Doc told me to eat healthy
Home grown with less fat
And since nowhere near wealthy
I'll start by eating the cat

Empty Boxes

Empty boxes stored away
In case needed some distant day

They sit around forever ignored
Forgotten since they were stored

The day after their removal's completed
Is the day you find that one is needed

The Donkey & the Elephant

An elephant and a donkey met,
    on the road one day
They stopped for a chat,
    before they went on their way
The elephant told the donkey
    just how strong he was
The donkey said he could work all day,
    without a break or a pause

They talked of how they saw the world,
> while each kept grinning

Both said that without them,
> the world would stop spinning

Unfortunately, their discussion
> ended up in an all-out brawl

The moral of this story is simple
> and should be clear to all

Each thought himself important,
> who without the world couldn't fare

But the moon, stars, and clouds above
> didn't even know they were there

Firetruck

When I was just a little boy
It was my most treasured toy,

Now on a shelf in the antique mall
It's not considered a toy at all.

Old Friends

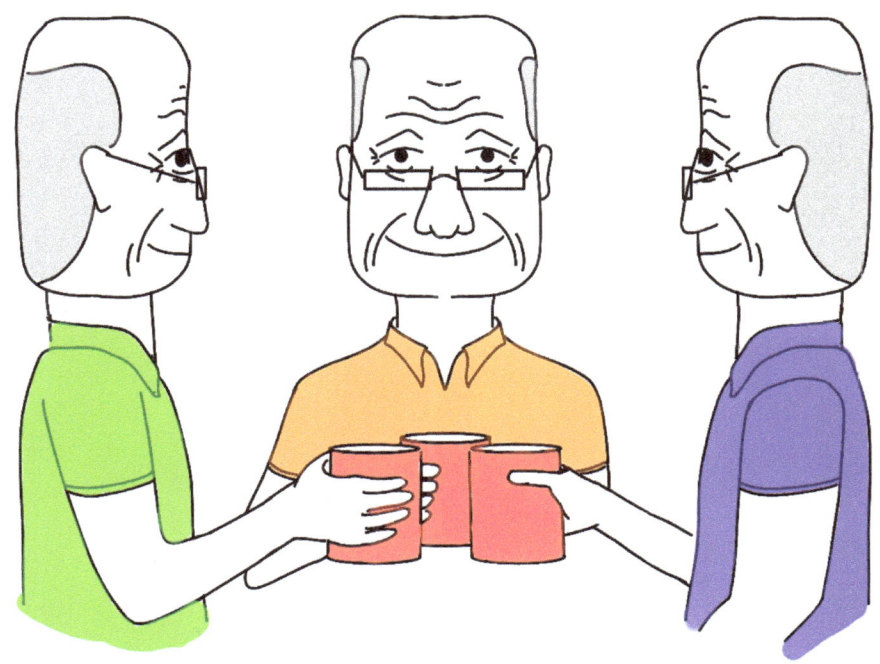

Old Joe Old Jerry and Old Ben

Have been together since when

They went and explored

Where dinosaurs roared

Long before they were old men

Grandpa's Stories

I thank you for letting me retell the story
Of long ago when I was in my glory

They were for me the most exciting years
Every day full of honor, love and tears

I may have told it to you once or twice
But that you let me tell it again was nice

It was polite of you not to say it was boring
But you made your point when you started snoring

Is it Fair?

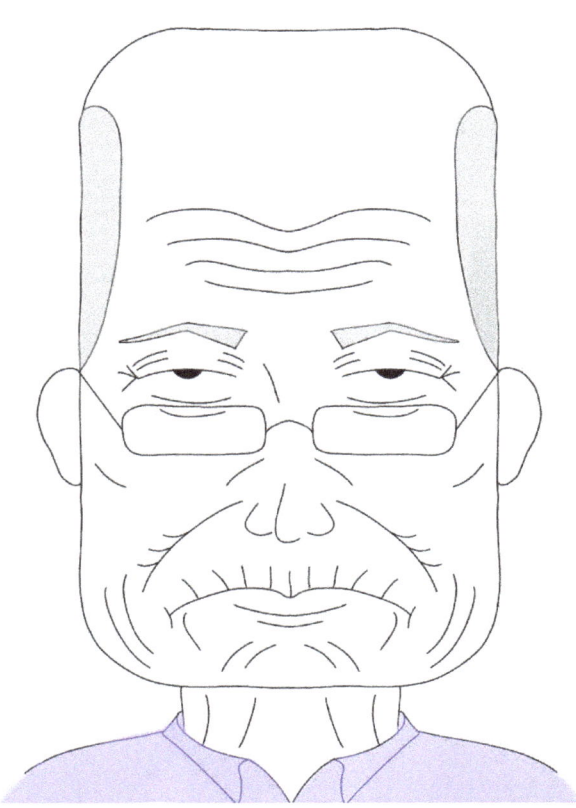

Sometimes I feel as old as time
My expectations are a little lower
But I think I get around just fine
Though my pace is a little slower

Why as the universe gets older
Its stars have all gotten twinklier
While as I've gotten older
I've only gotten wrinklier

I Look at the Stars

I look at the stars
They are so far away
But I know that I'll visit
At least one someday

Will it have beaches
Or mountains galore
Maybe I'll find
A large dinosaur

I look at the stars
And think just possibly
There is someone out there
Looking back at me

Sleeping Cat

Each morning's filled with new life
As I struggle to awaken from the dead
It's only after my first cup of coffee
That my mind is filled with dread

I slowly start to remember
That there is just so much to do
It's then I tell my sleeping cat
I wish I could trade places with you

I Want to Fly

Birds fly
Bats fly
I've even heard of flying fish

Insects fly
So why-oh-why
Can't I get this one wish

If people flew
Before you knew
All cars would go away

It's overdue
That our wings grew
I want to fly today

Lane in the Rain

There once was a boy named Lane
Who ran around nude in the rain
When asked by a Cop
He said he would stop
But when it stormed, he did it again

Muddy Shoes

He asked to play with his buddy
Mother said he had to study
He went to his room
To study she assumed
Later his shoes were all muddy

Sharing

I have a little sister
Who follows me all the time
She has lots of toys
But wants to play with mine

Before it's time for naps
We always read a book
She never reads her own
But at mine she wants to look

After getting in our beds
and she's quiet for awhile
She smiles peacefully while sleeping
I'm glad we share a smile

May's Queen

I dance spin and twirl
I laugh and have fun
Winter's gloom is over
I rejoice in the new warm sun

Leaves and flowers bud
The world is turning green
The sun is Spring's King
And I am May's Queen

My Hat

I wear a stocking hat when it's cold
And a baseball cap when it's hot
Hair always covered will fall out I'm told
But if you don't have any it will not

My Love Smiles

My love is loveliest when she smiles
She smiles her best enjoying her sleep
Many happy hours away she whiles
If she could only do it without a peep

My Belt

When my dog and I were out for a walk
I found what I was sure was the prettiest rock

I thought I'd take it to show my mother
When I had to stop for I found another

Next my dog pointed out one to me
It was really quite cute I had to agree

A fourth, a fifth, an eleventh, and twelfth
Both my dog and I were proud of ourselves

But on the way home embarrassment I felt
For I suddenly wished my pants had a belt

Lady Chesterfield

Morning's fog lingers
    As I try to wake
Thinking only of
    The coffee I'll make

But the sun would never shine
> The day never start

Without your smile
> That wakes mind and heart

Work days would be long
> Hard to get through

Without the knowledge
> I will come home to you

No matter what my burden
> I know that I can share

The troubles of my day
> While you listen in your chair

My First Fair

I went to see my brother, but he wasn't there
A note on his door said he'd gone to the fair

I've never before been to a fair is the truth
People selling what I don't need in their booth

Walking around the fair I saw all sorts of things
People selling vegetables, paintings and rings

I did not see anything for sale that I required
Let alone anything that in any way I admired

As I left for home my brother I never did see
I was amazed to find three full bags with me

Too Much Sun

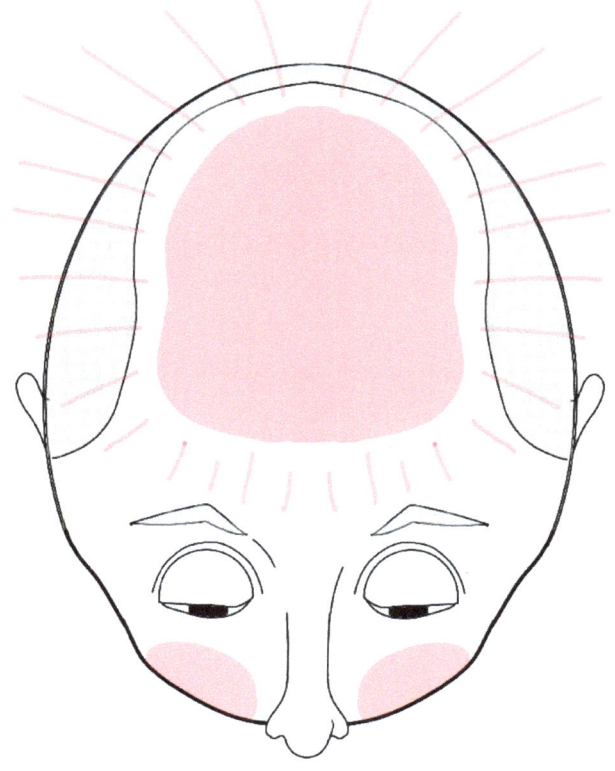

Today's a first
Now I must admit
I'm losing my hair
For from the sun, I've been bit

Peanut Butter

I would loudly proudly utter
My love of peanut butter
Telling all that it is the perfect food
But my mouth is temporarily glued

Who Taught Him That?

I got ready to watch the game
With all my loyal friends that came

Before the game began, we agreed
Our team will surely win indeed

With the first score we all rejoiced
But from the back a boo was voiced

With the second score a round of applause
And another dissenting boo there was

It was after that booing that I began
Thinking one of my friends was not a fan

I could no longer focus on the game
I had to know on who the booing to blame

They score so the culprit I hoped to be viewing
I saw in the back it was my parrot that was booing

Neighborhood

I know my neighborhood really well
    Every alley, hill and even smell
I know each dog on every stoop
    Every garage where there's a hoop
I know each and every apple tree
    Every bush to sneak a pee
I wonder when I grow and move away
Will I know my new neighborhood as well someday

Penguins

All penguins look alike
As far as I'm concerned
Each chick hears the difference
Their mother's call they've learned

All politicians look alike
As far as I can see
It's hard for me to hear the difference
They all cry "Vote for me"

No Longer Lonely

One more lie to spare my feelings
One more lie because you care
Your lies no longer leave my heart reeling
For I know there is no love there

This is not your last lie I fear
I must do what is best for me only
I see my courage in the mirror
knowing I'll be alone but no longer lonely

(_ _ _ _'s) Prayer

Now I awaken,
> from my sleep

At my desk,
> work in a heap

If I should nap,
> again today

I pray you Lord,
> keep the boss away

Rude Awakening

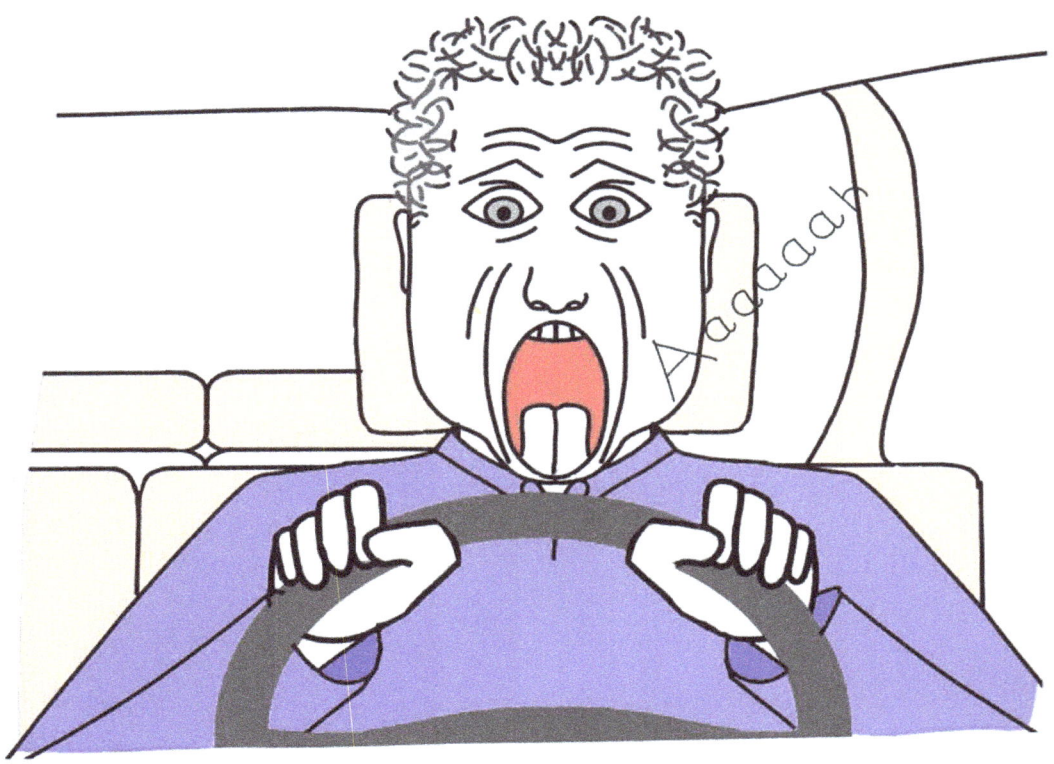

Sleep suddenly appears
    As silent as a mime
It filled me with fears
    For I was driving at the time

Shoes

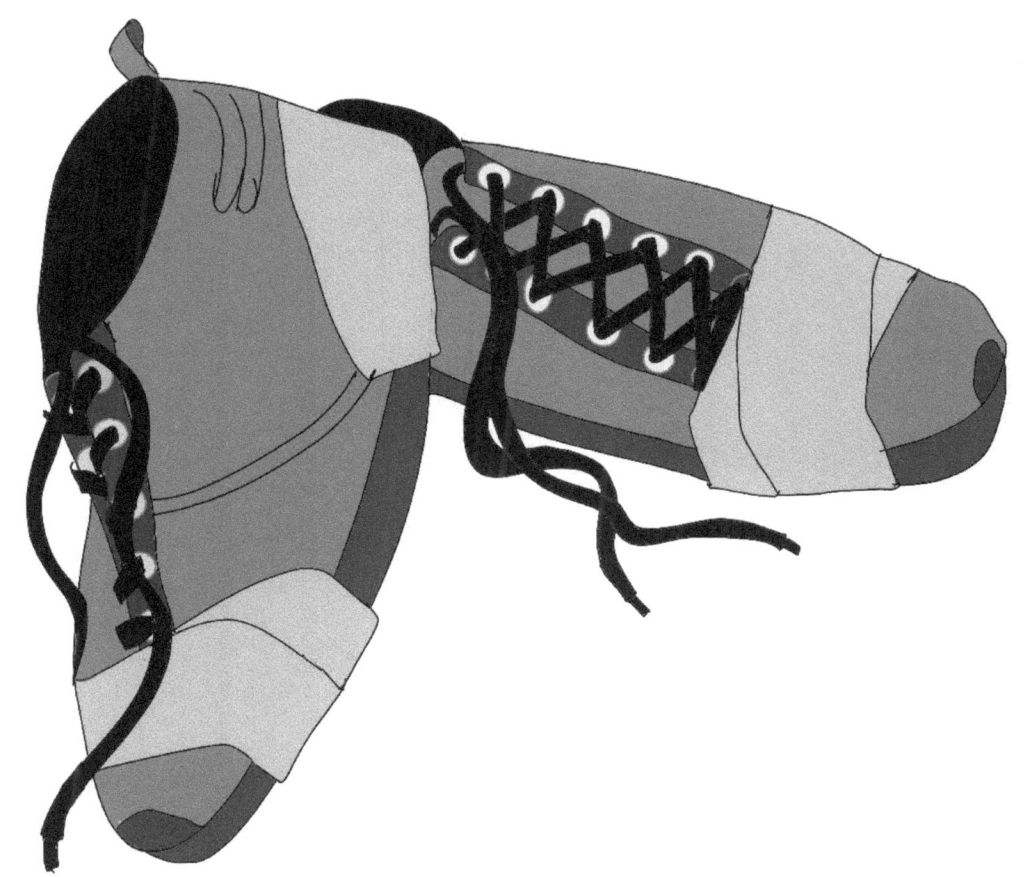

Oh, my tennis shoes are comfortable
Although well-worn and stained
The duct tape makes them invulnerable
Unless it has snowed or rained

Scary Eyes

From small white seeds
> grow the giants of my garden

Spreading faster than weeds
> in a living orange green tartan

I like them in stews
> most like them in pies

But everyone's favorite use
> Is the one with scary eyes

My Shadow

I see my shadow at daybreak
    It looks so strong and tall
I know it's the shadow I make
    But it's not like me at all

They say I'm short, I'd have to agree
    And I'm not that awfully strong
But my shadow's made by me
    So how can my shadow be wrong

My Kitten

My little Siamese kitten
Considers herself a queen
She thinks it only fittin
Since her licking keeps her clean

She gives a smile to all
As she strolls around the house
Then coughs up a furball
That used to be a mouse

Sharing

I raised my daughter to share with others
Even if only her annoying brothers

I hoped she would pass this lesson on
To her children and hopefully beyond

Sadly, my grandkids she never told
They didn't need to share their cold

Getting Older

The older I grow

The more I learn

The more I learn

The less I know

Socks

My brother had on different socks
    One was orange, one was blue
His answer to why left me flummoxed
    He said one was old, the other new

Be an Example

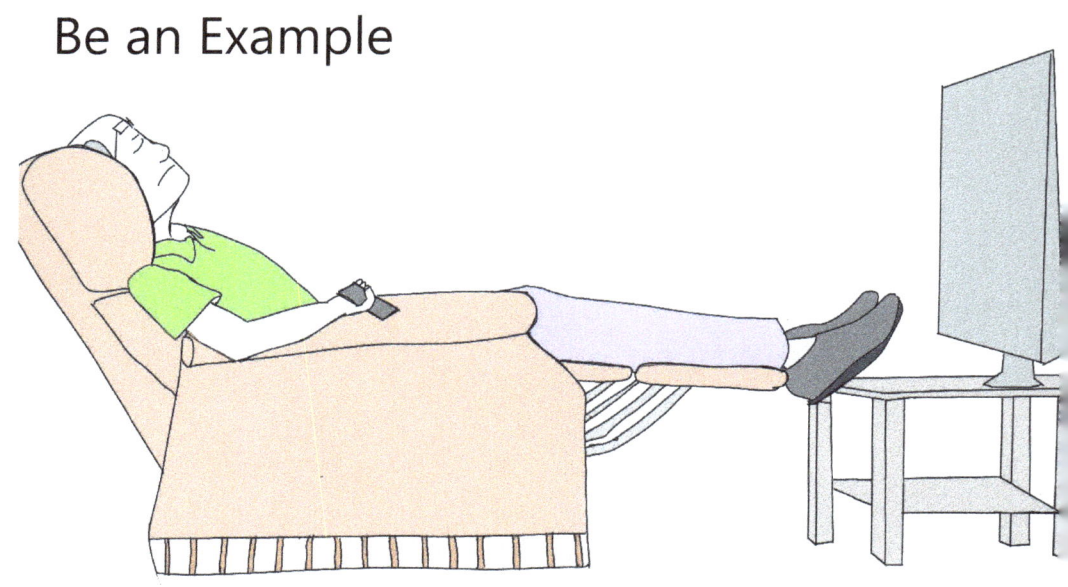

Why play solitaire or shop on TV
Why read mail sent to addressee

A life worth living takes some effort
Break out of the flock and become a shepherd

All parents be they young or older
Are examples of a life that's active or a placeholder

You may think your actions only impact you
But memories of them last long after you're through

Sunrise

The sunrise breaks the slumber
Of the restful in great number
But there are a few who choose
To roll over and hit snooze

A Belt

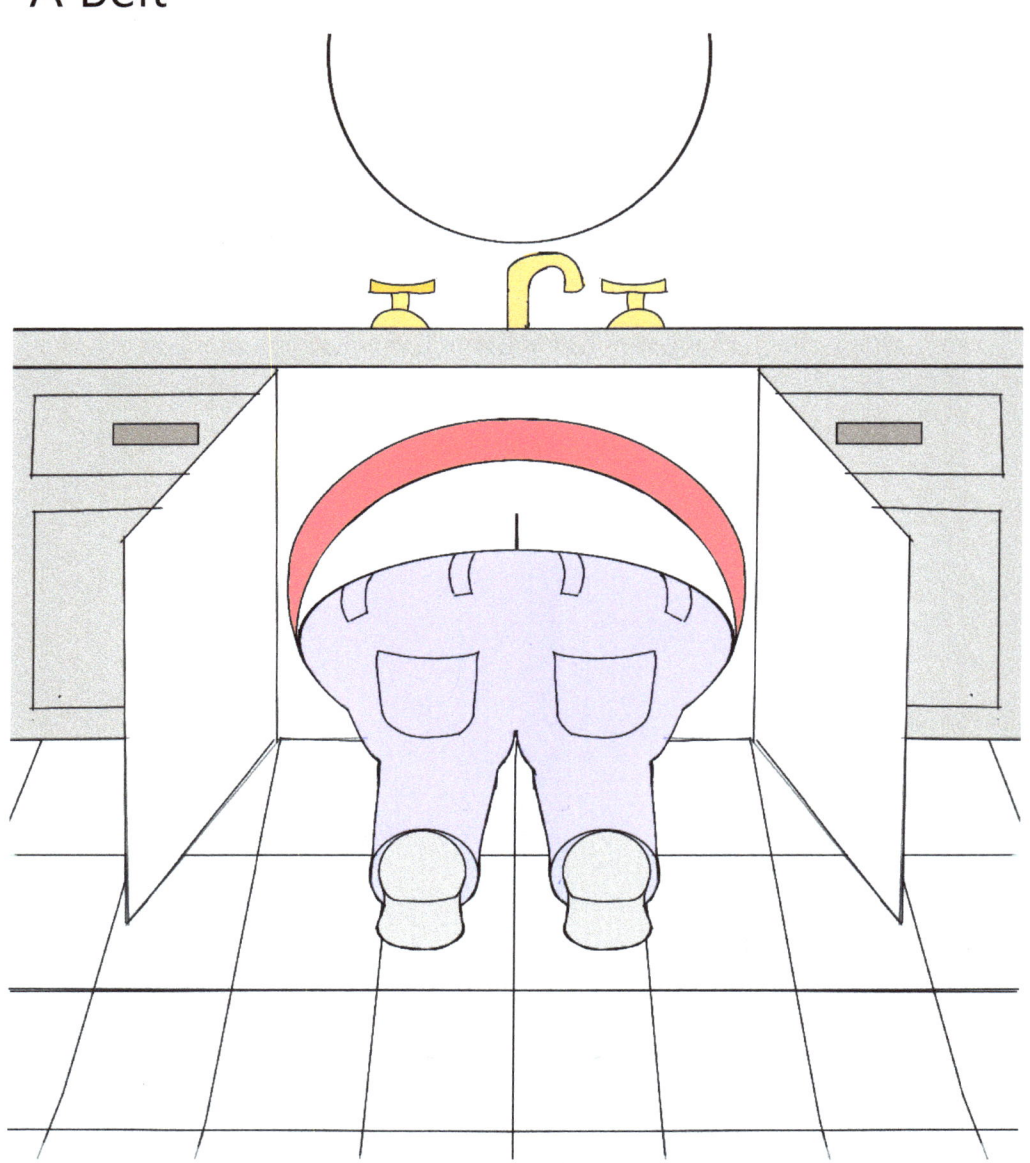

I don't know if you're aware
Your pants have slipped
And your bottom is bare

It's not something that should be shown
To anyone outside of your own home

A belt this problem could have blocked
Keeping your privates private
And the public from being shocked

If belt and suspenders both fail
You might try a shirt with a longer tail

Another Plea

I only stopped for one drink
I was only going to have a beer
Judge I hope that you don't think
It's my fault that I ended up here

My boss at work is a fool
My wife just doesn't understand
Judge if you only listen you'll
See it's their fault that I am on this stand

The cop was out to get me
There was a bee inside my car
Judge I beg you hear my plea
My record doesn't deserve this scar

Those other times weren't my fault either
Please don't send me to the pen
Judge this experience has been a teacher
I promise you'll never see me again

Eulogy?

They say being old made him grouchy
But he had been that way since birth
On every subject he was touchy
He enjoyed tirades like others do mirth

Some made excuses for his behavior
Saying deep down he had a good heart
But to those who truly knew him
He was just a cantankerous old fart

He began getting his affairs in order
For he had started thinking of his demise
He asked all that knew him to give his eulogy
But found none that would tell that big of lies